SUNRISE COAST

Colne Point to Lowestoft Ness

VOL 2 The Coast in The Past Series
ROBERT SIMPER

Published by Creekside Publishing

ISBN 0 9538506 3 3
Copyright Robert Simper 2002
Printed by Lavenham Press Ltd '
Lavenham, Suffolk

Robert Simper has always lived and worked very close to the tidal estuaries of East Anglia. This is his thirtieth book and although many of these cover rivers, coasts and boats all over Britain, his passion for the East Coast always leads him to return to this subject. He has also contributed to many other books, notably three chapters in *Chatham, Inshore Craft* and has written regularly for two nautical magazines. He was a founding member of the River Deben Association. As a young man he became fascinated by Thames barges, and as a way of repaying the barge world, became chairman of the Dawn Sailing Barge Trust which is rebuilding the barge *Dawn*. He is a member of Anglia Authors, an association of authors and independent publishers promoting special interest books.

Cover Laden barge *Edme* at anchor in Pyefleet.

Contents

Introduction

The alarm clock went off at 2.30am and there was a muffled voice from the far end of the cabin saying indignantly 'it's too early'. But time and tide wait for no man and we had to move the boat out of the Brightlingsea Smack Dock. Going on deck we found it was nearly high water, but it was still dark. We hardly spoke as we ran lines out and hauled the 34ft bawley *Mary Amelia* clear of the other craft and out into deep water. It was the sort of manoeuvre where things could go horribly wrong, but we got clear and moved down Brightlingsea Creek and out into the River Colne. By then the sun was rising over the coast to the east of us, outlining the smacks and yacht masts against the first light. Out in the River Colne we let the anchor go and returned to our bunks for the rest of the night.

We could have been in another century that night, with the sight of the masts of smacks and barges gathered for a race, outlined against the sky, but with daylight reality returned to our lives. This was 2002 and we were sailing a traditional boat for relaxation, not to earn a living. The *Mary Amelia* had been built in 1914, making her one of the last working sailing boats built, but in her lifetime the coast had changed completely. In the Victorian and Edwardian period the rivers of north Essex and Suffolk had been commercial highways, alive with fishing smacks, barges and the rest, but at the beginning of the twenty-first century there is very little commercial traffic on the smaller rivers. The estuaries between Lowestoft and the River Colne have become recreation areas for yachts; only the Haven Ports inside Harwich Harbour and Lowestoft remained important commercial ports.

The East Coast rivers are different places to different people. The yacht racing fraternity does not see the estuaries in the same way as bird conservationists or the commercial shipping world, yet the physical coast is exactly the same. Any record of this coast has to try to reflect the many widely differing activities that take place. My English Estuaries series attempted to cover the history of the East Coast rivers, but time moves on and the aim with this book is to talk more generally about the boats, places and people on this fascinating low-lying English coast.

When I was growing up the bleak wind-swept Suffolk coast it was never called beautiful. Our Suffolk eyes were not opened until people from London started to move into the villages and rave about how attractive it all was. It is difficult to define the difference in character between Suffolk and Essex, but it does exist. However the maritime history of this stretch is virtually the same.

My way of trying to identify with this coast was by taking photographs. The shots of the barges *Alan* and *Cabby* at Felixstowe Dock in 1953 are my early attempts at photography. I had cycled there with friends from my home at Bawdsey, having taken the ferryboat to Felixstowe Ferry, and then cycling on to look at Harwich Harbour. We were all fascinated by the seaplanes landing, but for me there was the added attraction of the sailing barges in Felixstowe Dock. Felixstowe Dock was then a Victorian white elephant sitting alone out on the Landguard Marshes desperately fighting for economic survival. By embracing new techniques, and making use of its position on a deep-water harbour, Felixstowe has become Britain's major container port, even overshadowing the port of London. Back in the 1950s when we used to go into Felixstowe Dock for a drink in the 'Little Ship' no-one in their wildest dreams imagined that a major port was going to spring up on the wild marshes beside Harwich Harbour.

A few years later I visited Southwold for the first time. This was to go to a dance with a party of young people in the hall on the shore end of the remaining Pier. It was in the winter and I remember walking out from the warmth of the dance hall into heavy rain being driven in from the North Sea by a gale. At that time I thought Southwold was on the very edge of the civilised world.

Southwold, and Walberswick, across the River Blyth, became the Gem of the East, certainly as far as house prices are concerned. Southwold might have become world famous a little earlier, but just after World War II the local council firmly rejected Benjamin Britten's request for backing to hold a music festival. Southwold could not see the point so Britten talked Aldeburgh into hosting a festival and the rest is history.

Although there had been a modest leisure industry at Aldeburgh since the Victorian period, the town's main industry was fishing. The boats still put to sea from the beach in front of the town, but like everywhere else on the coast this has declined. When I first visited Lowestoft fish docks, one foggy autumn afternoon in 1957, the herring fleet was still there, but the count- down to its extinction had become irreversible. Back in the 1890s there had been lone voices crying that the North Sea was being over-fished, but for another fifty years the Great Autumn Herring Fishery went on relentlessly until most of the herring shoals were all but gone.

The Shingle Coast of eastern England, where the first rays of sunrise appear, is very vulnerable land. In the wild winter's gales the sea comes roaring over the tops of the offshore sand-banks and smashes down the soft sandy cliffs and sweeps the soil down the coast. This sand and shingle is always on the move, nothing is ever safe. Not just a few bungalows on the cliff tops are at risk from rising sea levels, it is just about all of East Anglia. Coastal defences are a necessary evil because they are, in reality, defending places considered far inland at present.

The horrendous problem of rising sea levels on this coast is always in the background. Past generations can't be blamed for the vast amount of land which has already gone into the sea, but all those who love this coast have a responsibility to make certain it is saved for future generations. Changes will undoubtedly take place, but inappropriate actions taken in the name of economy and conservation are in very serious danger of destabilising the whole coast. The present coastal towns and villages, to stay nothing of all the good farmland and wildlife habitat, could not be replaced.

This coast remains a place where the waves crash on the shingle beaches, the tide creeps across the grey mud flats of the rivers and the winds sweep across the open marshes. It is beautiful and very therapeutic. That alone justifies its continual existence, but in our overcrowded island, space is our most valuable asset. The sea defences in the twentieth century proved that the sea could, when there was a will, be held back. It takes real determination to hold back the sea, but if this battle is not fought, all the places in this book will join Dunwich at the bottom of the sea and the North Sea will continue to move inland.

Sea defences are often not easy on the eye. The Dip at Felixstowe that I remember as a child, around 1949, with a shingle beach backed on to a grass cliff, is now a totally different place guarded by a massive concrete wall. Yet without these defences the houses on the cliff top would join the Roman fort under the sea. I knew this area well when my grandmother had a hut here. My family, who had noticed I was keen on boats, urged me to learn to swim. My attempts at swimming usually involved a great deal of time struggling to stay on the surface. I hated the cold water and it occurred to me, as I was washed up on the beach, that human beings were not really suited for marine life, unless they were in a boat.

I have drawn on my own observations for this book, but it would not have been possible without drawing on the knowledge and help from other people. On sailing barges I have to thank Andy and Jane Harman for allowing me to share their enthusiasm when they carried freights in the *Edme*. In 1962 John Birkin discharged the sailing barge *Cambria* at Fingringhoe Mill, the last sailing barge to carry a freight up the River Colne. Forty years later, as Quarry Manager at Priors, John Birkin loaded the next freight into a sailing barge when the *Edme* loaded a trial freight to see how she would sail loaded. Jim Lawrence told me about his early days in sailing barges before 1950 when they regularly poked barges up to Marriages Mill, while J.R.Steele told me of the final years of Colchester as a port.

John Milne, who worked in the Port of Felixstowe for forty-seven years, told me about the early days of the port when sometimes they had difficulties in finding the money to pay the workers at the end of the week. On Mistley I have drawn on one of Chubb Horlock's accounts to learn about the Edwardian days at the quay. In a way the Thames spritty barges have become symbols of a lost era of commercial sail. More views on the past have come from Jon Durant, Chris Packard of Oyster Yachts and Renee Waite of Pin Mill.

Peter Nichols of Shottisham heard many stories from his grandfather Sam and others of his generation about the Sandlings Peninsula, which reach back to the time when the Martello Towers were built. Comer Mead gave me details of a totally different, modern form of defence when the barge *Charlie Rock* delivered Norwegian stone to the Deben mouth. John White and Duncan Read also talked about the ever-shifting bar across the entrance of the River Deben. After medieval fish traps were found in Essex I had wondered if the posts, now eroded away, in the Rocks Reach of the Deben had been these traps. Duncan Allan of Suffolk Archaeology Unit made me aware of the possibility of a whole net work of them at Waldringfield.

Just up the coast Graham Hussey has watched the entrance of the River Ore move south and then back to the north. For details up river past Havergate to Orford, Ralph Brinkley, Robert Moore Ede and Mary Read were most helpful. Also Angus Wainwright of the National Trust pointed me in the right direction on Orfordness and Clare Foss of Aldeburgh Museum passed on much of the great knowledge she has gained about that lovely little coastal town.

In 1981, when cruising in *L'Atalanta* with our family, we were stopped at Southwold by the weather and while walking around came across the Southwold Model Yacht Regatta. I recognised that this was something unique, but it was over twenty years before I took a closer look. The last Southwold beach yawl, *Bittern,* fell to pieces on the beach near Southwold Pier in the 1920s. Eighty years later model beach yawls were still being raced on the Model Yacht Pond. Life-long enthusiasts Nigel Osmer and Peter Boult explained the intricacies of the Southwold Model Yacht Regattas.

On the editorial side, thanks to Diana McMillan. My wife Pearl has worked, as on all the others, with me on this project. Not least in putting up with my obsession with sailing to some difficult spots in order to photograph them and explore. I have spent a great deal of time looking at the tidal waters on the East Coast of England and trying to understand them.

R.S.   Ramsholt .

Source of illustrations. J.R.Steele 2, Peter Herbert 29, Douglas Went 5,18, Paddy O'Driscoll 12, Christian Knights 40,42, British Museum 32, National Trust 57, Carol Twinch 54, Robert Moore Ede 59,60, Aldeburgh Museum 64, 65, 84, 85, 86, John Goldsworthy 58, Graham Henderson 71, 74, Ernest Graystone 108, Comer Read 75, John Burl 88, Jonathan Simper 90, 100, Paul Bruce 101, John Cragie 94 Graham Hussey 78, East Anglian Daily Times 61, colour 4,   Robert More colour 21. The remaining photographs are from the author's collection and most of the recent ones have been taken by him.

bold's Point Felixstowe .

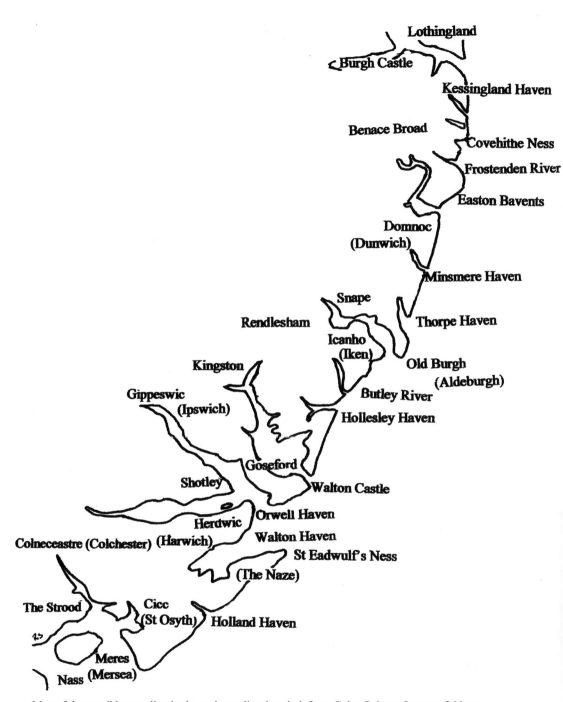

Map of the possible coastline in the early medieval period, from Colne Point to Lowestoft Ness.

North Essex and the Suffolk coasts under siege from the North Sea.

The sailing barge *Edme* leaving Mistley, 2002.

Chapter One

THE HAVEN GATEWAY

River Colne, Walton Backwaters, River Stour and the River Orwell

1. A barge with her 'gear' (mast etc.) down is about to be 'poked' up under the Hythe Bridge at Colchester to take wheat to the East Mills. To get under the two bridges called for precise timing and the barges, with a 'huffler' or mud pilot aboard, had to leave an hour and twenty minutes before high tide. Some barges with high bows had difficulties in getting under the Hythe Bridge. The *Millie* had the windlass bits sawn off in order to get under, while the *British Empire* had to have her boat full of water on the deck to 'keep the head down'. Once when Jim Lawrence took the *Mirosa* up to East Mill she got stuck under the second bridge and the elderly huffler climbed up over the bridge and went home. When he was returning in the early hours of the morning, on the next high tide, a policeman spotted him climbing over the bridge and thinking that he was attempting suicide the policeman grabbed him.

2. The British coaster *Adelphia* discharging, at Colchester, in 1989. In the 1970s and early 1980s when most coastal vessels were below 1000 tons the port of Colchester was booming. In about 1969 a new wharf was built at Wivenhoe and then another one across the river at Rowhedge. As ships became larger trade to the Colne fell rapidly. Wivenhoe closed in 1990 and Rowhedge in 1999. The last ship to discharge in the Port of Colchester appears to have been the 1,054gr tonne *Beveland* at Rowhedge in 1999 and an Act of Parliament closed the Port of Colchester in 2001 so that no commercial vessel can now discharge above the 1993 barrier. The wharf at Brightlingsea was built about 1983 and came to prominence in the Miner's Strike during 1987 when large amounts of Polish coal was discharged here and this became the port for the Colchester area.

3. The Colne One Design *Blue Peter* passing the Colne Barrier, 1994.

8. A horse pulling two barges near Swan Lock, Wormingford on the Stour Navigation in about 1902. The Stour Navigation, 24 miles from the tidal Stour up to Sudbury Quay Basin, was opened in 1717. The barges used on the River Stour Navigation were similar to those used in the Fens. Each 'gang' consisted of two 13ton barges that were towed by a horse. It took a gang a day and a half to go from Mistley Quay to Sudbury. Barges were used at Sudbury until 1916 and traffic to Clover's Mill at Dedham finished in 1928.

9. The Stour Navigation Trust's *Stour Trusty* running trips from the Quay Basin, Sudbury, 1985 which was part of the long campaign to reopen the Navigation. In 1968 the River Stour Trust Ltd was formed and this has campaigned for the reopening of the whole navigation. While a river without boats is totally dead, many residents of the Stour Valley have increasingly campaigned against the reopening of the whole navigation.

10. The bridge over the River Stour at Flatford in about 1910. The original bridge at Flatford was built in 1705 and in 1906, when the bridge was in poor repair, Hain Friswell campaigned to have a new bridge built in exactly the same style as the one made famous by John Constable. By the Edwardian era the Stour valley was becoming famous as the setting of John Constable's painting and people were seeking to preserve it.

11. Hire boat at Flatford in about 1920. Further up river, just below the road bridge at Dedham, rowing boats were hired out to summer visitors by 1900 and this became Dedham Boatyard. Between 1952-79 G. F. Smeeth was building wooden boats at the Dedham Boatyard. The largest craft Fred Smeeth built was the 33ft *Miranda* for Hervey Benham in 1960. He was working on the 20ft Dunwich beach boat when he died and this was appropriately called *Fred's Last.* In 2002 Cameron Marshall took on the lease of the restaurant and 25 rowing hire boats.

1. The bawley *Bona* and steel Mistley-built barge *Repertor* beating into the River Colne in the 30th annual Colne Smack and Barge Race from Brightlingsea, 2002.

2. The Essex smacks *Kate* and *Lizzie Annie* off Mersea Island taking part in the Dredging Match to mark the opening of the native oyster season, 2002. The Match is a competition, to keep old skills alive and see which smack can land the most oysters under sail with hand-hauled dredges. The smacks are on the Common Ground, but this side of the buoy is the Tollesbury & Mersea Oyster Co. grounds and to make certain none of the smacks strayed on their oysters a boat patrolled the boundary.

3. Andy Harman on the barge *Edme* and John Birkin watching the loading of 52 tons of ballast at the Ballast Quay, Fingringhoe, 2002. This was the first time a sailing barge had been loaded with a freight for thirty-two years. Priors donated the ballast, a firm which operates six vessels carrying 3000 tonne of ballast every week, from the River Colne to London.

4. The Royal Navy Type 23 frigate *HMS Grafton* in the River Orwell on a goodwill visit to Ipswich in 2001.

12. Green's Mill at Brantham, when the River Stour was still tidal, in about 1963. The last sailing barge to bring a freight up to Brantham Mill was the *Orion* in 1938 and in 1971 a dam was built at Cattawade to cut off the tidal waters.

13. Jack Lucas fitting out his duck punt at Manningtree in 1998. Jack Lucas built his first duck punt in 1947 when he was eighteen. In the old days these 18ft Manningtree punts, mounted with a gun rather like a small cannon, were used to shoot flocks of wildfowl on the River Stour in the winter. They were also used for putting out fishing nets in the creeks. Eventually the plywood punts were just built for racing, but were still sailed with a small lug or spritsail and steered with an oar. Manningtree is the last place in Britian where they are regularly raced. This is virtually confined to the Lucas family and old punts have been burnt to discourage outsiders from taken part.

14. The sailing barge *Resolute,* owned by Fred Horlock, taking advantage of a 'fair wind' up the River Stour. This was the era when ships were built and owned by local men for a particular trade to one port. Horlock's barges brought imported animal feed from the London docks to the Mistley mills.

Fred Horlock started with a quarter share in the barge *Pride of the Stour* and from this built up a fleet of sailing barges and steamers, some of which were built at Mistley. Between 1924-30 F.W.Horlock had seven steel barges built at his Mistley yard. This started with *Repertor* and ended with *Blue Mermaid* in 1930 which was the last true cargo sailing barge built.

15. The *Spithead* at Mistley in 1972. This coaster was built as a landing craft in World War I for the Dardanelles campaign. Shortly before this *Spithead* had been driven ashore at Shingle Street, but was hauled off the beach. She was being used to run ballast, dredged from off Wrabness.

16. Andy Harman loading the sailing barge *Edme* at Mistley with a token cargo of Edme flake wheat in 2002. This was a re-enactment voyage under sail to Green's Mill at Maldon. The barge *Edme* had been built by Cann at Harwich in 1898 and her original owner Richard Horlock named her after the company he hoped to get work from. However over a century later the barge and company were united in this voyage.

Before World War I there were often twenty barges lying at Mistley Quay, all discharged by day labourers known as 'quay lumpers'. There were seven pubs on the quay to quench the lumper's thirst. Before a suction elevator was installed in 1913 every bag had to be carried ashore on a man's back. Germain was reputed to have been the strongest of the lumpers and once, after work, rowed a boat around to Pin Mill, won a race and rowed back again. Another time, during the labour shortage in World War I, he discharged 1000 bags (75 ton) from a barge on his own in a single day. Each 76kg bag had to be carried down a plank into the Maltings and he then ran back. When there was no work unloading barges Germain went around the pubs tap dancing, he had clogs with farthings on the heel, while his mate Truck played a tin whistle. They used to say these men were strong in the arm, but weak in the head, but it was a very hard life even for a fit man.

17. The 45ft *Allison Theresa,* an inshore trawler, entering Harwich, in 2001. Built at Whitstable in 1970, she was the largest powered fishing boat ever owned in Harwich when she arrived there for her owner Fred Good that year.

18. The Sopwith's J Class *Endeavour II* racing off Harwich in 1934. Until 1939 the J Class yachts moved around the coast off Britain taking part in the major regattas. The Royal Harwich Yacht Club then had rooms in the Pier Hotel and regattas for the great yachts were organised from there. The *Endeavour II* had a paid crew of 19 and the owner, his wife and a few guests would have been aboard as well.

19. Lightships at Harwich 1974. Harwich is a base for Trinity House who maintain the buoys and floating lights off the coast of the United Kingdom. In the early 1970s most of the manned lightships were withdrawn from service and moored in Harwich Harbour until they were converted to unmanned lights or sold.

20. Felixstowe Dock, in 1953 with the barges *Alan* and *Cabby,* being discharged. Felixstowe Dock was built for Col Tomline in 1886 as part of his grand scheme created a new port around his Beach End Station. In fact the new Victorian resort town of Felixstowe grew up on the higher ground to the north. The Tomline's Orwell Park Estate, which covered much of the eastern side of the Orwell, passed into the Pretyman family and the Dock was a small scale affair with sailing barges and a few small steamers delivering freights for very local industries.

In the 1940s Mr Pretyman used to visit the Dock once a year, as if it was one of his farms on the estate, to be told how much income he would receive from it that year. All this changed in 1951 when Gordon Parker, a corn merchant from Stoke Ferry, bought the Felixstowe Dock and Railway Co. Post-war Europe had a tremendous demand for English grain and Parker had been shipping grain out of Wells on the Norfolk coast. The trouble with Wells was that ships could only get in on certain tides, and the attraction of Felixstowe was that ships could enter and leave Felixstowe at any state of tide or weather, a huge advantage.When the East Coast Flood of 1953 hit Felixstowe, the high tide over rode the river walls around the Dock and poured across the open marshes to drown 29 people in the Langer Road area. Many were drowned in a caravan site, the screams of those calling desperately for help still haunt those who remember that terrible night. On the Dock the former Ipswich Malting Company building was being used to store 'essential foods'. Because of the post-war food shortage the Government had kept stores around the country and released food whenever there was a food shortage. Most of these stores were destroyed by the Flood.

Felixstowe Dock struggled on, sometimes having a job to persuade the bank to let it have the cash to pay the port workers at the end of the week. Then came the National Dock Labour Scheme which gave the dockers in large ports a job for life. As no-one then had any incentive to move cargoes quickly there were many stoppages. The little port of Felixstowe was at the right place at the right time, with a deep-water harbour and a labour force that worked hard to turn around ships as fast as possible.

The London dockers originally refused to handle containers so Felixstowe was keen to capture this market. Gordon Parker, who travelled to his own little port in his Rolls Royce, liked to be in command and built the first container wharf, the Landguard Terminus, in 1967.

21. Barges just before the start of the 1972 Pin Mill Barge Match. From the left *Ardwina*, *Gipping*, *Remercie*, *Convoy*, *Dawn* and behind the *Lord Roberts* setting sail. Thirty years later only the *Ardwina* was still sailing from this group.

22. Mick Lungley, race office, at the Pin Mill Barge Match in 1992. Mick Lungley had gone into the Ipswich sailing barges when he left school and in 1956 he became skipper of Cranfield's *Venture* bringing Manitoba wheat, imported into the Royal Docks, London up the coast to Cranfield's Mill at the head of Ipswich Dock. After five years with Cranfields he moved to R & W Paul's barge *Marjorie*. Freights on this sailing barge included taking malt from Ipswich Dock down to the Royal Albert Dock for export. He was later master of a coaster until he left the sea and became landlord of the 'Limeburners' at Offton.

23. 'Splodge' Duke, mate of the sailing barge *May*, the day after his final victory in the legal battle against double mooring charges on the River Orwell, 2001. The foreshore and riverbeds of the East Coast are under various ownerships and the riverbed of the River Orwell, since a series of charters from the medieval kings, belongs to the Borough of Ipswich. In the 1990s over 400 yacht owners, in the Orwell were charged for their moorings by both the Ipswich Port Authority and the Borough of Ipswich. Derek Moore and Alistair Duke refused to pay the second charge and were taken to the High Court in London by the Borough of Ipswich. The High Court ruled that Ipswich Borough owned the riverbed, but the right to charge for moorings had become vested in the Ipswich Port Authority.

24. Sailing barges and square riggers in Ipswich Dock about 1910. The barge on the right is the Mistley *Marjorie*.

25. The paddle steamer *Suffolk* coming into the New Cut berth at Ipswich about 1924. The London and North East Railway steamers *Norfolk*, *Suffolk* and *Essex* used to run pleasure trips between Ipswich, Harwich and Felixstowe.

26. The Mistley built barge *Repertor* and other craft lying at the Common Quay, Ipswich Dock about 1953. The mills at the head of Ipswich Dock became the last place to be regularly used by sailing barges to deliver freight. They brought imported grain from the London Docks and took back flour to the Thames and the Medway.

27. The Ocean Youth Club craft arriving at the Custom's House during Maritime Ipswich 1982. The Wet Dock was opened in 1846 and it transformed Ipswich from a country market town into an industrial centre. The Victorians were very proud of their Dock and it had a promenade and bandstand near the lock gates, but as the area became industrial the town turned its back on the Dock. By the 1980s industry around the Dock began to move away and there were discussions about filling it in to make a lorry park. The purpose of Maritime Ipswich was to draw the town's attention to the fact that the Dock was an asset to be kept.

28. The courtyard behind the 'Neptune Inn', in Fore Street, Ipswich in 1985. This house, with its oak-panelled rooms, is a merchant's house dating from the 1400s. Now part of the Wet Dock, this area was the trading centre of Ipswich with merchant's houses backing on to quays along the River Orwell.

Richard Cobbold in his novel 'Margaret Catchpole', published in 1845, stated that the 'Neptune Inn' was the meeting place for smugglers in the late eighteenth century, but it was not converted into the 'Neptune' until later. However it may have been used by smugglers because a bricked off area in the cellar, according to legend, was that entrance to a tunnel which led to a nearby church. By the 1930s 'Ye Olde Neptune Inn' was the drinking place for quayside labourers and whole quayside area of Tudor Ipswich was very run down. In 1958 there was a Royal visit to Ipswich and the Fore Street area was smartened up, but by then the 'Neptune Inn' had closed and then was reopened in 1972 by Peter and Margaret Horsman as Neptune Antiques.

29. Aboard the schooner *Annie Davey* at Ipswich, loading fertilizer for Bude, North Cornwall. Captain G.H.Johnson is third from the right and in the foreground is the schooner's huge kettle to provide tea for the loading gang. At sea these kettles remained on the galley stove for the voyage and more tea was added from time to time. The Ipswich fertilizer trade had grown out of the coprolite diggings along the Sandlings coast.

30. The New Cut, Ipswich, 1903. The original course of the Orwell ran through the present Ipswich Dock, past the Tudor merchants' warehouses, but when the Wet Dock was constructed in the 1840s the New Cut was dug to allow the fresh water from the Gipping to flow out into the Orwell.

31. Wrinch's barge *Snowdrop* at Stoke Bridge about 1906. Stoke, at the first narrow point of the tidal Orwell, was the ancient river crossing place. The fresh water Gipping, flowing down from the heart of Suffolk, formed a delta of channels above Stoke. The barge traffic up the Gipping Navigation to Stowmarket was not regular. Horses were hired from a carter at the 'Bull', a public house behind the Custom's House, to tow the barges.

Chapter Two

RIVERS THROUGH THE MARSHES

Rivers Deben, Alde/Ore and Blyth

32. This photograph shows the excavated outline of the 84ft long Anglo-Saxon longship in Mound One, at Sutton Hoo in 1939. This excavation, largely carried out by local archaeologist Basil Brown, revealed a great warrior with all his treasure and personal effects. The burial took place around 625 and is assumed to be Raedwald, King of East Anglia. This great burial only survived as one end had been removed and when grave robbers dug down into what they thought was the centre they missed the burial chamber. All the other mounds in the burial field had been robbed. In 1860 Mr Barritt, the farmer at Sutton Hoo, dug into Mound Two, but found it empty. However it was the Sutton warreners Will Collins and his mate King, alone on the heath in the winter just before World War I, who dug most of the mounds in search of rabbits and kept objects they found.

33. Martin Carver, Director of the Sutton Hoo Research Project, explaining the excavation in Mound Two to a BBC camera team and David Attenborough in 1985. At Sutton Hoo two great warrior leaders were given ship burials in Mounds One and Two, but Mound Two had been almost totally destroyed by grave robbers. It is probable that Mound Two contained the burial of a warrior with a 60ft ship.

34. The Duke of Edinburgh, being shown the Sutton Hoo excavations by Martin Carver in 1987. The burial field on the hilltop at Sutton Hoo was probably used between about 600-630, presumably by the Wuffing dynasty who had their great hall at Rendlesham.

35. The excavation of the 'young prince and his pony' in Mound Seventeen with the remains of Mound Two in the background, 1991. At some point, probably during the food shortages in the Napoleonic War, the burial mounds had been ploughed and the smaller mounds levelled. The Research Project, which began an archaeological exploration of the site in 1983, left a slight bump near the track until the last weeks. This bump, Mound Seventeen, turned out to be the only mound the Project dug which had not been robbed.

36. Chris Topham of the Suffolk Archaeology Unit excavating the second Anglo-Saxon grave field, discovered in 2000. This grave field was in the kitchen garden of Sutton Hoo House and on the present site of the National Trust's Interpretation Centre and car park. The second grave field proved to be earlier than the royal burial mounds on the hilltop, although exactly where these people lived is yet to be discovered.

37. Building the Anglo-Saxon houses at West Stow, 1979. While Sutton Hoo is a glimpse of the world the kings of East Anglia belonged to; West Stow is a similar vision of the ordinary village life. This tiny settlement on the edge of the Fens was buried in a sandstorm. After excavation a replica village was build on the site of the original houses.

38. **Left:** A Lynx helicopter from the Army Air Corp, Wattisham removing a boat hulk from Bloss' Island, Melton in 1997. The upper Deben became a dumping ground for old boats and houseboats, and although many people liked the wrecks others campaigned to get them removed. Bloss' Island, sometimes called Flea Island, is a patch of saltings at Melton that got its name from Melton cattle dealer and farmer Fred Bloss. The Bloss family were connected with the far older droving trade. Cattle were driven down from Scotland, which usually took about a month, then after 1780 a three day Bullock Fair was held at Melton in which farmers and grazers from all over East Suffolk and Essex came to buy Scottish cattle. These were large events and in 1816 over 6000 cattle were sold here. Later when the cattle had been fattened on the grazing marshes along the Suffolk coast they were brought to Melton and then drovers walked them to the London Markets, usually in about a week. Even after the railways came droves of sheep were driven into Melton to be sold at a fair near the church, until this sale petered out after World War II.

5. The *Grand Turk*, replica of an eighteenth century Royal Navy frigate, arriving at the Common Quay outside the Custom House in Ipswich Dock, 2000.

6. Capt. Richard Woodman's *Andromeda* and other classic yachts gathering to lock into Ipswich Dock, 1998. They were arriving for the Maritime Ipswich Rally. The first of these periodic events was held in 1982 to heighten the town's awareness of the usefulness of the dock. It was the beginning of two decades in which the Ipswich Dock turned from being part of the commercial port into being developed for leisure use.

7. The 49ft Holman and Pye designed Oyster yacht *Ocean Scout* beating into Harwich Harbour. The Oyster Group was started at West Mersea in 1973 by Richard Matthews and has grown to be the best known builder of large sailing yachts in Britain. Every year between 30-35 new hulls are produced in moulding yards at Wroxham and Colchester and these are taken to Fox's Marina at Wherstead Road, Ipswich for completion and launching. From here yachts go to owners all over the world.

8. Des and Liz Pawson in their workshop, at Wherstead Road, Ipswich. When the Pawsons moved to Wherstead Road in 1976 it still backed on to the River Orwell and they kept a boat on the mud at the back. In 1981 the West Bank Quay was constructed cutting them and Fox's yacht boatyard next door off from the tidal water. Des started doing rope work in the Scouts and always did it as a sideline, but after receiving a mass of orders at the Shotley Festival of the Sea in 1989 they decided to become full time craftsmen in ropes and knotting. At the bottom of the garden is their unique Museum of Knots and Sailor's rope-work.

9. Jonathan and Richard Webb on Pin Mill hard with Geoff King, waiting to float the steel barge *Melissa* up on to wheels so that she could be taken up to the Webb's yard for rebuilding, 2001. The 'Butt and Oyster', once the only house at Pin Mill, was probably built after a landing Hard was created here. Certainly Pin Mill Hard was there by the late seventeenth century and was further improved to celebrate Queen Victoria's Golden Jubilee.

10. The steel Mistley-built *Xylonite* in Webb's Dry Dock, 2002. This dry dock was the cause of a bitter local dispute. Barges have been repaired and owned at Pin Mill since the middle of the nineteenth century, but in 1993 the new residents in this waterside hamlet put pressure on the Council to remove the dry dock from the hard. Since the 1930s numerous sailing barges and other craft have become houseboats at Pin Mill and then abandoned by their owners, turning the foreshore into a jumble of rotting timbers, a sight which is loved by some and hated by others.

11. The spritty barges *Reminder* and the *Thistle* in Harwich Harbour, 2002. The *Reminder* was built by Fred Horlock in his yard at Mistley, in 1929.

12. The Felixstowe Volunteer Coast Patrol Rescue Service's *Volunteer,* John Cresswell coxswain, coming ashore to her base on Cobbold's Point after pulling a yacht off the Andrews Spit, 2002. John Cresswell started this service in 1997, because the Coastguard withdrew the inshore rescue boat he had been operating. At weekends in the summer the *Volunteer* goes to the aid of swimmers and vessels in difficulty in the Felixstowe area. Between the breakwater in the background and Cobbold's Point, are the remains of Mr Cobbold's Pier.

39. The Simper's sucking herd turned out, from Brian Bloss' lorry, on to grass for the summer on the Dairy Farm marshes, the only remaining grazing on the Bawdsey Level, 2002. The grass marshes along all the East Coast were a very important part of the local economy because with East Suffolk's low rainfall and light land the top land could not support grazing animals in the summer, while the marshes with their high water table could. In the 1953 Floods all East Coast grazing marshes went under salt water. To justify the expense of repairing the river walls the Government put pressure on farmers to plough up the marshes for wheat. In the 1990s the environmental concerns led to some grass being reinstated, but there is a real threat to the marshes by rising sea levels and indifferent flood defences. It would be impossible to prevent all flooding, but if these marshes are lost to farming or wildlife they can't be replaced. The pressure on space for human activity in eastern England means there will not be space to set up wildlife reserves if the existing ones are lost.

40. A sailing barge laden with cement from Kent entering the Ferry Dock, Woodbridge, 1928. The flat-bottomed barges could get right up to Woodbridge, but the deep draft schooners had to off load part of their cargo into lighters at Kyson Point. The flat-bottomed barge went right up to the wharf at Wilford Bridge and there is a kind of folk memory that goods were once moved in punts up the freshwater river. The legends such as ships going up to the treacle mines and cattle being shipped down from Kettleburgh Dock were treated as a joke, but they may just be a memory of some ancient traffic.

41. The sailing barge *Dover Castle*, and a small steamer discharging in the Ferry Dock, Woodbridge about 1922. The *Dover Castle* was the last barge trading on the river. Captain Skinner used to sail down to Bawdsey Ferry, load shingle on the bar knolls and take it up to Woodbridge for either building the Woodbridge By-pass, now part of the A12, or for sale to local builders. After this until about 1946 Ted Marsh ran the ex-lifeboat *Iron Duke* for ballast from the Deben. After Skinner's death in 1935 the *Dover Castle* was run up on the mud under the Ferry Cliff, Sutton, where its remains still lie, while the *Iron Duke's* hulk lies on the old river wall opposite Melton Dock.

42. The 31ft cruising yacht *Dawn* just after the bottom was painted on the Ferry Cliff, Sutton about 1930. The *Dawn* was built at the Lime Kiln yard, Woodbridge by A.V. Robertson in 1921. From the 1780s there seem to have been a few yachts built and kept at Woodbridge. Ebenezer 'Khartoum' Robertson, a Scot who played the bagpipes and ran a Barge yard at Ipswich, spotted the Lime Quay yard for sale when he went through by train to collect rents from properties in Southwold in 1884. He bought the yard, where merchant schooners were built until 1853, and established yacht building here. His son 'Bertie' Robertson took over running the yard with his brother in law Everson, but they fell out and in 1899 Everson started boat building at the Jetty and coal yard below the Ferry Dock.

43. The water wheel at the Woodbridge Tide Mill was powered by tidal water caught in a pond, now the Woodbridge Yacht Harbour. Built in about 1795, when it finished grinding in 1957, this was the last working Tide Mill in Britain. In the foreground is one of the Whisstock 4-tonners.

44. Yachts laid up by Whisstock's Boatyard at the Tide Mill Quay in 1952. River pilots sheeted the weather-boarded mill in corrugated iron, just after World War I, in between other jobs. Claude Whisstock converted the millpond into a yacht harbour in 1962. In 1976 the Kember family bought the yacht harbour and in 1994 began to dredge out the silt and pile the banks.

45. Before the sale of the Woodbridge Tide Mill in 1968 Claude Whisstock said if he bought it he would pull this 'eyesore' down and extend his yacht yard. However R.T.Gardner asked his wife Jean, over breakfast one day, what she wanted for her birthday and she said 'Woodbridge Tide Mill.' The Gardners purchased the Mill and gave it away for preservation. What had been an eyesore became a treasured tourist attraction for Woodbridge.

46. Above Right: The yacht *Kimbark* just before she was launched off Whisstock's yard. Claude Whisstock was a noted builder of wooden yachts, and like most of the Woodbridge boat builders, he hated the idea of fibre-glass yachts and would not build them, although the yard did finally turn to aluminium-hulled yachts. By tradition after a launching the youngest apprentice on the yard used to present the owner's wife with a bunch of flowers. There was nearly an embarrassing incident at a launching in 1956. An apprentice was just about to present the owner's mistress with a bouquet of flowers, as she was the woman that he had seen visiting the yard with the owner, but Claude Whisstock moved swiftly and diverted the presentation to the right lady.

Whisstocks closed in 1990 and the yard was operated between 1992-95, by the Woodbridge Boatyard & Slip Co. They concentrated on repairing large craft and hauled out the 75ton 6ft.6in draft *Deben Glen,* then the largest yacht hauled over a slip on the Deben.

47. Right: A Woodbridge boatman returning passengers from a trip on the river, 1906. The Woodbridge shop-keepers used to have rowing boats and row their families up or down the river in the summer, according to the tides. The first recorded yacht race on the Deben was in 1784 when the *Templer* and *Flora* raced down to Bawdsey Ferry. The event was recorded because after the race one of the yachts was stolen, but was returned later. Woodbridge attracted 'gentry' residents, after it had been a garrison town in the Napoleonic Wars, and they wanted to develop the river for leisure. In about 1898 the warehouses on the southwest side of the Ferry Dock were demolished and a promenade path was made along the river wall to Kyson Point.

50. The *Winifred*, a steamer with sails to 'take the weight of the engine', loading cement at Waldringfield in about 1904. On busy days 400 tons of cement were loaded here. The Waldringfield Cement Works was opened in 1872 and closed in 1907. A small barge, *Kingfisher*, was used to bring mud from Hemley Point up to Waldringfield Quay where it was baked in 'kells'(kilns) with chalk, brought by barges from the Thames quarries. Mason, owner of the Waldringfield Cement Works, had seven sailing barges that brought chalk and coke from the Thames and returned with cement. In 1906 the first village regatta was held and in 1921 the Waldringfield Sailing Club was started. After this the riverside area turned from industrial use to leisure.

48. Above Left: Melton model boat maker Ian Dunmore with the Suffolk yawl *Black Joke*, made by John Cragie at Southwold in 1920, on the Kingston Model Yacht Pond, Woodbridge, 2002. Model yacht racing started on the Round Pond, London in 1820 and racing model Suffolk yawls began at Lowestoft in about 1885. The original Model Yacht Pond at Woodbridge was built by public subscription in 1935 and was later enlarged.

49. Left: Paul and Jo Masters celebrating the restoring of their gaff yacht *Clytie* at Shotley Festival of Sail, 1993. The *Clytie* was built at Woodbridge in 1922 by Everson's and for almost the entire career of this yacht she has been based in the Deben. Jo is the fifth member of her family to own the yacht. Since the 1970s there has been a very strong movement on the East Coast to rebuild wooden boats of character.

51. A tiller steered stackie barge on the beach at Waldringfield in 1911 with one of Mason's barges loading cement at the quay. The stackie barges sailed to London with a stack of hay half way up the mast. When the skipper was standing at the tiller he could not see where he was going, so the mate had to stand on the stack and shout directions. The Church of England used to make a charge when the barges were loaded on the fore-shore. Waldringfield Cliff, which was fenced off with iron railings to prevent people from damaging it, used to be Church of England glebe land until 2001 when the ownership changed to Waldringfield Sailing Club and the twenty-seven hut owners.

52. The Lower Ham Tips buoy with Stonner Point in the background on the River Deben above Waldringfield. Aerial photographs taken of the Deben in 1941, probably as part of the planning for the anti-glider posts that were put across the ooze mud, show lines of stakes in V shapes on these mud flats. These appear to have been the remains of medieval fish traps, lines of 'wicker fences that guided fish into a trap. These traps were used in all the estuaries but were such a problem to navigation that an Act of Parliament banned them in 1605. By 2002 the ooze on the flats has eroded away so that there is little trace of the posts.

Stonner Quay was built in about 1860 to ship out coprolite. The digging of coprolite, which was ground into phosphate, was very important to the Sandlings villages in the Victorian period, because it gave work to the men when they were not needed on the farms. The work was done by hand and once a gang working in the pit near Sutton Hall unearthed a clay pot of Roman coins. They clubbed together and sent one of their gang to London by train, but he did not know where to sell the hoard and returned without any money to share out. The men kept a coin each, but then handed the hoard over to the farmer at Sutton Hall who reported the find.

53. The River Deben Association's first litter collection in 1992. Every autumn the Association's members have collected up to 4 tonnes a year of rubbish from the tide-line. An indication of the popularity of the Deben, but the mess and damage on the foreshore is one of the least favourable impacts of the leisure activities on the river.

54. The 'Arms' at Ramsholt Dock about 1911. The original 'Dock Inn' was just up the road, but in around 1900 Lord Rendlesham, aware of the growing number of people coming into East Suffolk on holiday by railway, adapted the Dock Farmhouse into the 'Ramsholt Arms Hotel'. Because it was considered a hotel, not a public house, the 'Arms' was unique because it did not have any pub sign until 2001. In the 1930s there were only a few moorings off Ramsholt Dock so that seaplanes from Felixstowe Dock sometimes landed for 'anchor tests'. Their crews then rowed ashore for a drink in the 'Arms' tiny bar.

57. The Duke of Edinburgh can be seen landing on Orfordness in about 1961. From left to right- behind the Duke are Robin Fenton, Reg Partridge, Bob Boot, Wally Green, Aubrey Buxton and Alan Carr.

55. Above Left: A gang of men repairing the river wall on the Ramsholt Dock Marshes, between the Ramsholt 'Arms' and the church, after the 1953 Floods. In 1953 an abnormally high tide swept over the sea defences in Eastern England creating serious loss of life and tremendous damage to property. On the East Coast time is measured not in great world events, but bad gales and major flooding.

56. Left: A group of local film extras outside Ramsholt Church in 1994. The Anglo-Saxon and medieval villages were around the church, but the last of the cottages were pulled down in about 1964. No new houses have been built in the village since 1904.

58. Above: Tom Brinkley's fishing smack *Juno* sailing RAF mechanics from the Orfordness airfield up to Slaughden, in about 1917.

59. Above Right: Ralph and Peggy Webb sailing the Bombay Tomtit *Nadya* at Orford in 1952. Webb's *Nadya*, Pelly's *Hebe* and Craig's *Sandpiper* have been raced regularly in the Tomtit class at Orford Dabchicks Sailing Club. In 2002 the *Nadya*, built by Ernie Nunn at Waldringfield in 1929, was one of four Tomtits still sailed and raced at Orford.

60. Right: Ralph Webb's Bermudan yawl *Gudgeon* sailing past Orford Quay with George Brinkley standing on the deck, 1955. In the background are Quay House and the MOD crane. The *Gudgeon* was brought back in bad order and rebuilt by Peter Wilson at Aldeburgh in 2000.

62. Ralph Brinkley, Harbour Master for the New Orford Town Trust, 2002. The Orford Town Trust owns the riverbed of the River Ore from the parish boundary with Sudbourne down both sides of Havergate to the mouth, while the riverbed of the Butley River belongs to the Greenwells. Ralph's father Victor was also Harbour Master, but it was not until his death in 1960 that Ralph came 'down on the river.'

61. Left: Stuart Bacon at the door of his Orford craft-shop while the Royal Armouries seized an 11ft bronze Spanish cannon, 2001. Since 1971 Stuart Bacon has organised underwater explorations on Dunwich, the city under the sea. A wreck on the Dunwich Bank was also investigated and in 1994 this cannon was raised. There then followed a lengthy legal dispute over the fate of the cannon and finally the Receiver of Wrecks ordered, because it was a rare type of cannon, that it should be removed from Orford and taken to the Royal Armouries Museum at Fort Nelson.

63. Aldeburgh 'cod banger' smacks laid up at Slaughden Quay, Aldeburgh in 1906. The Suffolk ports had been involved in the Icelandic and North Sea cod fishery since the medieval period, but originally the fish were salted before being brought back. The nineteenth century Aldeburgh and Harwich smacks had 'wet wells', a tank in the centre of the hull filled with sea water through holes in the bottom, and the catch was brought back alive.

64. The village of Slaughden in about 1904 before it became part of 'washed away' Suffolk. It is said that on a high tide the twenty-two houses at Slaughden had their front doors opened to let the sea water run through the house and out of the back door. The white 'Three Mariners' had a whale-bone sign over the door, that had been brought back from Iceland on a cod smack.

On the right, hauled up in front of Ward's Shed, are the gigs used by the pilot companies. The Aldeburgh pilots, who mainly put pilots on ships bound for London, were divided into two beach companies that were very bitter rivals. About 1850 the North and South look-out towers were built as headquarters by the rival 'Up-Towners' and 'Down-Towners' companies. The North Tower, built by the Aldeburgh Beachman's Salvage Co, was later taken over by the Fisherman's Guild and then the RNLI.

13. Bawdsey Ferry in 1999, aboard the *Sae Wylfing*. In calm waters *Sae Wylfing,* can make seven knots under a single square sail, when reaching. She can beat against the wind, but it is possible that it would simply be quicker to row up-wind.

14. The 44ft *Sae Wylfing* off Green Point in the River Deben, 1999. The original full size longship found at Sutton Hoo in 1939 did not have a mast step, it had probably been removed to make way for the king's burial chamber, but she appears to have been straightened aft to take a side rudder. The *Sae Wylfing,* a half size replica of the original long ship found in Mount One, was built for Edwin Gifford because he wanted to prove that she could sail as well as be rowed.

17. The 86ft motor yacht *Ginger Dot* with Tammy Grundy's workboat attempting to haul her off the old Whisstock slipway, 2002. The *Ginger Dot* later floated off on the night tide, with the help of another fishing boat. The *Ginger Dot*, a wooden, American motor yacht built in 1922, was used by the aviator Charles Lindbergh in the unsuccessful search for his kidnapped son. The *Ginger Dot* was a houseboat at Melton when she was bought by Sue and Angus Brown and taken to Whisstock's yard to be rebuilt.

From the Elizabethan period wooden merchant ships were built at Woodbridge, mostly launched at the bottom of Lime Kiln Quay Road. Claude Whisstock launched his first craft, the 35ft motor cruiser *Bendor*, at his new yard in 1932 and building continued there until the yard closed in 1990. The *Ginger Dot* was likely to be the last major piece of wooden boat building at Whisstocks Yard. A bitter battle was going on between the purchaser of the site, who wanted to build housing, and the Suffolk Coastal District Council who wished it to be developed as a water front amenity for the town.

15. Above Left: Seamus Heaney and Kate Sussan, the National Trust Property Manager, at the opening of the National Trust's Sutton Hoo Interpretation Centre, 2002. The Dublin-based poet Seamus Heaney had not visited Sutton Hoo, but was asked because of his translation of the 'Beowulf'. This Anglo-Saxon poem covered the burial of a great king and seems to be very similar to the Sutton Hoo pagan burials.

16. Left: The 84 year old Woodbridge boatyard owner Frank Knights decided to retire in 2002. He trained at Robertsons and when returning from the Royal Navy in World War II started the boatyard on Ferry Dock in 1947. Initially the yard built beach boats for longshore fishing and pleasure launches before concentrating on repairs. Wooden boat building was revived between 1992-4 when four open boats were built, ending with a 14ft Kestrel dinghy in 1999, but Frank kept the Ferry Dock as a berth for wooden and traditional boats.

18. Yachts in front of Waldringfield Sailing Club after the fiftieth annual Procession, 1997. The Procession is unique to the River Deben and is on the Sunday at the beginning of the Deben Week regatta. Yachts, dressed overall, come up the river to attend a church service on the beach at Waldringfield. This was started by Trevor Waller, vicar of Waldringfield and a keen sailing man, because the Church of England then owned the foreshore and he thought this was one way of getting yachtsmen to attend a church service.

19. John White on the Felixstowe to Bawdsey ferry boat, 2002. After an apprenticeship at Fox's, John joined Trevor Moore building open workboats at Felixstowe Ferry Boatyard. John took over running the ferry after over forty years in the Felixstowe Ferry Boatyard, using one of the boats he had built.

65. View of the 'Model Yacht' pond at Slaughden in about 1908. The pond, given by Dr Elizabeth Garrett Anderson, was dug to entertain the children of summer visitors, but it quickly became popular with adult 'sailors'. In 1940 this pond was filled in and after World War II a new pond was built near the Moot Hall. In Aldeburgh Carnival the children's Egg Boat Race takes place on the pond.

66. A spherical mine that had been trawled up by a fishing boat the day before exploding in the River Alde below Iken in 1996. About a decade before, a similar mine was blown up off Waldringfield on the River Deben. During World War II the East Anglian coast had massive defences against possible invasion with mine fields off the coast. Mines were put on the beaches and army camps and anti-aircraft batteries stood on the high ground. Only a few overgrown pill boxes and very occasional mines are the reminders of that grim period in the coast's history.

67. Crescent Shipping's *Bencol* being discharged at Snape, 1972. After Swonnells closed, Snape Maltings was sold to George Gooderham. Aldeburgh Festival then leased some of the maltings for their new concert hall, while the rest of the maltings was developed for warehousing. However in 1971 a small craft shop was opened in the workshop on the quay and after this a very genteel form of tourism took over.

69 The tools of the malster's on a malt floor, now the Tea Room, at Snape Maltings, 1966. Snape was a floor maltings where, in the winter, barley was soaked in water, allowed to germinate and dried to produce malt for brewing beer. All the work was done by hand until mechanisation made this process of malting too expensive. In 1965 S.Swonnell & Son went into voluntary liquidation which put forty-two men out of work. Many families had spent two and three generations working at Snape Maltings and the sudden closure hit the village very hard. At this period the farms and local industry, which had employed large numbers of people, were forced to mechanise. This changed the character of Suffolk. Local people used to live and work in the countryside but gradually more people from cities and towns came out to live in the countryside and began commuting to the towns for work.

68. Left: The Southwold boat *Kerry Louise* being re-launched at Southwold Harbour after a refit in 1981. The open clinker boat was the workhorse of the Suffolk coast from the Anglo-Saxon period until grp hulls became general in the 1980s.

Chapter Three

THE SHINGLE COAST

Landguard Point to Pakefield, including Southwold.

70. The opening of Simon Read's 'The Forgotten Fleets' on The Dip Sea Defences 1995. Sea Defences, although very necessary, are often rather brutal intrusions on the landscape. These wall motifs were intended to take the harshness off the concrete walls. Simon and Ros live on the Dutch barge *Jacoba* at Woodbridge.

71. The hamlet of Felixstowe Ferry seen in 1894. To reach the Ferry across the Deben the lane went straight past the front of the 'Ferry Boat Inn' and across the marshes. When Sir Cuthbert Quilter, the London financier who built Bawdsey Manor, started the chain ferry in 1896 the landing was placed on the shingle spit which had built up. The old landing became buried under landfill on which the Felixstowe Ferry Boatyard stood. In the 1990s this area became the subject of a lengthy legal ownership dispute with the Felixstowe Ferry Foreshore Trust.

72. Rebuilding the river defences in front of Felixstowe Ferry Sailing Club in 1989. The Quilters had built a groyne on the point to protect their ferry landing. This wooden barricade held the shingle and created the point the Felixstowe Ferry Sailing Club was built on to such an extent that they had a dinghy park in front of the club house. The pressure of the tidal water forcing its escape from the Deben tears away the foreshore at Felixstowe Ferry. A process that environmental engineers predict will increase and be irreversible, taking much of the hamlet, if the Government plans to flood a large area of the Deben valley ever becomes a reality.

73. Maurice Read's ferry boat *Mayflower* landing at Felixstowe Ferry in about 1955. The Bawdsey ferry then ran from the beach downstream from Bawdsey Quay to this point, where the Quilter Groyne was then buried under the shingle. In the background are the radar masts of RAF Bawdsey. The last of these masts was collapsed in 2000 and replaced by a smaller mast.

In the inter-war period the British Government asked Sir Robert Watson-Watt to look into the possibilities of developing a death ray. Watson Watt found little hope of developing death rays, but realised that every time a plane landed at Heathrow he got a blip on his screen. To investigate this further the Government stationed Watson-Watt and his team out on the marshes at Orfordness and then on to Bawdsey Manor to develop radar. Radar pylons can be seen in Bawdsey Manor grounds. The discovery that these Chain Home transmitter towers sent out radio waves that bounced back and showed up any flying aircraft was found just in time for it to be vital during World War II.

75. The 3000 tonne barge *Charlie Rock* bringing rocks into the River Deben in 2001. Because erosion threatened Felixstowe Golf Club and the sailing club two breakwaters, built of 4-6 tonne Norwegian rocks, were constructed on the southern shore of the River Deben entrance in 2001-2. The ship that brought the rock from Larvik, Norway, anchored off East Lane and the rocks were transferred into the 268ft (82m) barge *Charlie Rock*. This barge, piloted in by Felixstowe Ferry fisherman Duncan Read, was the largest vessel ever to enter the Deben. The *Charlie Rock* only loaded about 1000 tonnes but drew two and a half meters (8ft) of water but she had 65ft (20m) beam. Near the port hand buoy the channel was only 82ft (25m) wide. She often touched the bottom when she came in on the flood tide so that the tugs dragged her through the shingle. Normally the barge was brought in stern-first about an hour and a half before high water and as many rocks as possible were thrown on to the shore, but as soon as the tide turned she had to go out with the first of the ebb tide. In all some sixteen trips into the Deben mouth were made.

74. Left: The beach at Felixstowe Ferry at the mouth of River Deben, 1893. Some of the fishermen were then keeping their boats on the beach in front of the Martello Tower T, which was then a Coastguard Station. Just in the centre is the galley *Pride of the Deben* which the local fishermen operated for salvaging. In the 1880s Albert Passiful and the Ferrymen earned some lucrative salvages with his galley. Just before the World War I *Deben*, with Newson as skipper, went out to ships ashore on the Shipwash Sands. The *Deben* came back loaded with cutlery, a piano, and whisky and by the time they reached the Ferry some of the men were lying drunk in the bottom of the boat.

76. A.P.Waller in a duck punt on the shingle knoll in front of Bawdsey Manor at the mouth of the River Deben, 1889. The London financier Sir Cuthbert Quilter bought up most of the land between Shingle Street and the Deben and started building Bawdsey Manor, but discovered that the sea was eroding away his estate. Between 1880 and 1936 the Bawdsey Estate had a Beach Gang putting up and maintaining groynes.

77. In 1996 the 28ft Felixstowe Ferry fishing boat *Pauline* hit one of the shingle knolls at the Deben entrance and rolled over and sank. At one time Duncan Read was transporting the catches from the thirteen boats landing at Felixstowe Ferry, but in 2002 this number had fallen to six boats. In 2000 Craig Ablitt's fishing boat *Our Bless IH314* was the first new boat to join the Felixstowe Ferry fishing fleet for nine years. This boat, mainly intended to fish for sole off the Deben, was one of two grp Kingfisher hulls that were fitted out by Andy Moore and Craig Ablitt. The other hull was Nigel Gain's *Onward HH55*.

© G.Hussey 2002

78. The Boathouse Point at East Lane, Bawdsey in 1907. Within five years all this had gone into the sea. According to a legend in Bawdsey 'men once drove cattle past the present East Lane beach to graze on marshes' which suggests that there had once been a considerable amount of land in front of the present point. As the Boathouse Point gave shelter from the prevailing south-westerlies in the Victorian period the Bawdsey fisherman launched their boats, which included a salvage galley, from the Shingle Street side. In the 1920s Dutch engineers were employed to construct the 'Prom' to defend East Lane. In 1977 the German coaster *Harle Strand* went ashore on East Lane point, after engine failure. Unfortunately, although the coaster was towed off undamaged, her weight had damaged these coastal defences. Although repairs would only have cost a few hundred pounds at the time, the authorities refused to do it because 'it was not worth it.' The defences deteriorated and in the 1996 northerly gales the sea almost broke through. A great deal of money had to be spent transporting rocks from Northampton to defend Bawdsey.

79. The green house at East Lane had arrived in kit form as part of Quilter's plan to create the Edwardian holiday resort of Bawdsey-on-Sea. Headlands such as East Lane are constantly eroded away by the force of the tide pushing south. From just north of Great Yarmouth this tidal drift moves shingle south. This shingle builds up and creates bars across the river mouths and the tide escaping from the rivers forces channels through the shingle knolls. These channels change constantly, but the major changes take place in the winter gales. The offshore sandbanks reduce the size of the waves, but north-easterly gales, coming all the way from Norway, will force the sea right over these banks on a big tide. When the full force hits the coast it creates havoc and causes erosion.

80. The Martello Tower and World War II gun emplacement at East Lane in 1979. The great storm in 1996 washed away the land from under the gun emplacement and revealed many covered World War II anti-invasion defences. These defences, although quite small, are vital to this area of the coast because if the sea could get behind them then the whole village of Bawdsey and part of Alderton would eventually go into the sea.

81. Martello Tower on the Alderton Marshes with the Buckanay and Shingle Street towers in the background, 2002. Over the centuries, since the Romans built forts overlooking the entrance of the River Deben, the Suffolk coast had been defended against possible attack from European powers. Several times during the nineteenth century a state of cold war existed with France and Martello Towers were built as a deterrent against attack. The twenty-nine Martello Towers between St Osyth and Aldeburgh were built from 1808-12 with bricks, probably made at Grays, and landed on the beaches by sailing barges in the summer. The Martello Towers each had a cannon, which had a range of up to two and a half miles but because of marsh fever (malaria) they were probably not garrisoned. However officers quarters were built in Bawdsey, away from the marshes, and there were barracks in Hollesley and Shottisham. Many of the roads, on the Suffolk coast, were straightened by army engineers during this period, so that the troops could be marched quickly to fight off any foreign invasion.

82. The Coastguard Cottages at Shingle Street in 1972 with boats hauled up on the beach. There was another Martello Tower to the north of these houses, but it was demolished when the river mouth moved south. The beach settlement at Shingle Street appears to have started in the later part of the Napoleonic War when the Royal Navy used Hollesely Bay as an anchorage. The fishermen appear to have moved south from Aldeburgh and Slaughden, although their boats were built in Woodbridge. The original squatters' cottages were built of driftwood from ships wrecked on Orfordness. Before 1939 Shingle Street men made a precarious living fishing, wildfowling and loading barges with shingle. Some new houses were built just after World War II to replace the ones destroyed in bombing practice.

83. An 18ft Aldeburgh beach boat, 1901. As it is summer time and the boat has a trawl aboard, it is probably sailing back up the coast to trawl back down on the tide. The sailing boats seldom worked more than three miles away from the landing. In calm weather the Suffolk boats were rowed, but they sometimes used a drawsail, a square sail, which was put into the water and the tide dragged them along.

86. Landing cod on Aldeburgh beach in about 1928. Middle and right are Fred 'Dodger' Gooding and Sam 'Shakey' Ward. At this time drift net fishing for sprat and herring were the main fishery, long lining for cod did not become so important until the 1950s. The Aldeburgh fishermen switched to retailing fish from the sheds they built on the beach and by taking the retail price they were able to survive on the small quantities of fish landed.

84. Above Left: The Sprat Dinner at Aldeburgh, held either in the 'White Lion' or 'Victory' until 1906, was modelled on the Colchester Oyster Feast and was intended to promote the sales of sprat. At Aldeburgh and Southwold sprat was the main inshore fishery and the large quantities landed were mostly sold smoked. The smokehouses at Aldeburgh were in Crab Street and at 'Cottage Industry' in Church Street. In 1921 the Aldeburgh Fisherman's Trade Guild was formed and they created a smokehouse where Aldeburgh Boatyard now stands. About 20 tons of salted or smoked fish were sent away each day, in the Guild's two lorries and sometimes they hired railway trucks. In 1946 the Guild bought a larger smokehouse in Oakley Square and at times the work of packing the fish went on through the night. In the 1950s the pattern of fishing changed and then declined. Aldeburgh became a holiday and retirement centre of music lovers and sailors, mainly from Greater London.

85. Left: Shaking the sprat out of the drift nets on Aldeburgh beach near North Tower in 1939. The boat belonged to Jack Pead and from left to right are Percy 'Putter' Taylor, 'Moose' Fisher and Tom Parnell. In 1930 there were 200 men employed, in the autumn herring season, in the boats working off Aldeburgh beach. The Suffolk beach boats were a local type of boat involved to suit the form of fishing. Because the men were used to sailing boats they used to take the engines out during the herring season because they believed they would taint the fish. When the tide turned they shot the drift nets and then drifted back so that they hauled the nets near Aldeburgh. After a good haul the boat was loaded so that only one plank was above the water, and then the boat was rowed ashore. Because of the difficulties in hauling the boats up the beach they tried to land them on the ebb tide. It took six men on a capstan to drag an 18ft boat up the beach. The older men came down to help for a 'feed of fish.'

89. Aldeburgh beach with two lifeboats in about 1985. About this time there were twenty-seven boats working off Aldeburgh beach in the summer and twelve in the winter. The Suffolk custom of painting the top plank blue or red sprang from the fishermen's habit of dropping into the lifeboat shed and 'borrowing' half-used tins of paint. In the bad weather landing on an open beach is very dangerous and many boats get 'overwhelmed' at some stage.

87. Above Left: Aboard Billy Burrell's Aldeburgh beach boat *Boy Bill* in about 1954. Left to right Peter Pears, E.M.Forster, Benjamin Britten and Billy Burrell. Aldeburgh was a successful fishing and merchant centre in the medieval period and in 1568 claimed to have 1300 fishermen and 130 sailors, but the Dunkirk pirates and erosion hit the town badly. The Moot Hall stood at the back of the town with five streets and a wide beach between it and the sea. Serious erosion started in 1590 and the first groynes were built to the north of the town. The erosion continued and it was not until after World War II that considerable sea defences saved Aldeburgh from the fate of Dunwich. Britten's Aldeburgh Festival gave the town a new purpose.

88. Left: Aldeburgh fishermen manning the capstan to haul the Aldeburgh lifeboat No 1 *Abdy Beauclerk* back up the beach in 1956. Once hauled ashore she would be turned around on a turntable to be re-launched bow first. By tradition the Suffolk boats are always turned clockwise. To go 'against the sun' is thought to bring bad luck.

90. The fishing boats hauled ashore in front of the fishermen's huts and early bungalows on the Brenthills, Thorpeness, 1918. Fishermen only took to using the beach after the Thorpe Haven, which had its entrance near Haven House, was closed when the tide dragged shingle across the mouth. All that was left by the Victorian period was just a gully with a wooden Shatterbone footbridge over it. A storm in October, 1911 washed away land on the Ness and many coins, dating back to the Romans, were found suggesting that there had been a considerable settlement on the Ness. The high tide broke over the beach and flooded the Thorpe marshes and Glencairn Stuart Ogilvie, who was developing a holiday village here, thought it would make a good boating lake for children. Ogilvie had Thorpeness Meare dug and this was opened in 1913.

92.Right: All Saints Church, last of the Dunwich Churches to go into the sea, on Dunwich Cliff in 1903. Every year the sea ate away more of All Saints until 1919 when the last of the towers was pulled down. The Victorians thought Dunwich, 'the lost city on the sea bed' was a wonderfully nostalgic place, but people had fought very hard to try and stop it from going into the sea. The townspeople of medieval Dunwich had put up faggot fences to protect the foot of the cliffs from the full force of the waves. However when the Wool Trade declined there was no cash to pay for these simple defences. The medieval walled town and the natural harbour of Dunwich went piece by piece, storm by storm into the sea. Once Dunwich had been a Christian centre of East Anglia and a major port, but when this was destroyed people abandoned the Suffolk coast. The population continued to fall until the railways brought back the first tourists and took local produce to the markets in the big cities.

95. John 'Young Dusso' Winter beside one of the Gunhill cannons, 1989. A former fisherman, sometime Mayor of Southwold, John Winter has been a great defender of the town's unique charm and resisted many proposed developments.

96. Cannons on Gunhill, Southwold in about 1900. The first cannons were given to Southwold in the 1630s to protect the town from the Dunkirkers, French privateers, and these were replaced, after complaints that the town was poorly defended, by the present 18-pounders by George II in 1745.

97. The author's young family in the Southwold Sailors' Reading Room on the East Cliff, Southwold, 1970. The Sailors' Reading Room was built in 1864 to provide a place for fishermen to spend the evenings instead of the public houses.

98. In the Victorian period the fishermen's village, wooden sheds used as boat gear stores, were at the bottom of the East Hill, Southwold. Seen here in about 1895 before they were washed away.

20. Yachts waiting at low water for the tide to rise at the River Deben bar to give them enough water to go out to sea, 2002. The Bar Buoy was then at its most southerly point, off the Dip almost down to the ruins of the Roman Walton Castle. It was also very shallow with less than a meter over the bar at low water spring tides and throughout the summer, on average, at least one yacht a day went aground while trying to cross the bar.

21. The Aldeburgh RNLI lifeboat *Frederick Cooper* being launched off her trailer, 1994. The Mersey Class *Frederick Cooper* replaced the RNLI Rother class *James Cable* in 1993. The *James Cable* was kept out in the open and was launched down greased skids. She was the last of the old type of pointed stern Norfolk and Suffolk lifeboats on station.

22. The Squib Class racing in Slaughden Quay Reach on the River Alde during the Aldeburgh Regatta, 2002.

23. Dragons racing in the Aldeburgh Regatta. Aldeburgh Yacht Club was started in 1897 and as the estuary is very exposed there is usually a very good sailing breeze.

99. Storm damage at the Gunhill, Southwold in October 1905 when the beach village was finally swept away. Southwold has escaped the worst erosion because piers were constructed at the harbour mouth, in 1752. The force of the shingle being dragged along the beach by the coastal tide drift appears to have been slowed down by the piers. In the early nineteenth century the wooden groynes were constructed to protect the beach. After the 1905 storm more serious defences were begun and this continued in the 1930s, but the situation was not stabilised until the construction of the 1952 reinforced concrete wall. However, since the sea continues to eat away the land either side of the town, this is not a long-term solution to the erosion problem. Suffolk badly needs an active policy to minimise the rate of erosion. In the past groynes and concrete walls worked well, but they have gone out of fashion. Rock breakwaters and offshore reefs seem to be the latest approach and since they have proved successful on other parts of the English coast should work on the shallow Suffolk coast.

100. Southwold punts hauled out below the Sailors' Reading Room about 1910. The Southwold boats, were known as 'punts', because they were almost flat bottomed. Most of the Southwold beach boats were kept on the beach until World War II. They were then moved into the harbour so that the soldiers would have a clear line of fire at any invading force. After the war the boats, then nearly all fitted with engines, found it easier to work from the harbour and the beach eroded away forcing most of the remaining boats away.

101. The wooden barque *Idun* was driven ashore on the beach in front of Southwold in a gale on January 17, 1912.

102. Peter Boult with his model beach yawl *Roaring Forties* at the Southwold Model Yacht Regatta, 2002. Peter was commodore of the Southwold Model Yacht Club for twenty-five years and the *Roaring Forties* is one of the older boats taking part. Like several of the other models the *Roaring Forties* was made by one of the Southwold beach fishermen about 1930. The model yacht pond was built by the pier company and is particularly successful because it is exposed and always gets a good breeze.

103. Covehithe Cliffs looking south to where the sea is eating around behind Southwold, 1997. Covehithe, with over a meter of the cliff going every year, is the erosion 'capital of the east.' Erosion is not an entirely natural situation, global warming and offshore dredging for aggregate have placed the coast under far greater risk from the sea, and there is a good reason to fight back to prevent it happening.

104. Beach End, Kessingland looking towards Benacre Ness in about 1910. On the beach are the fishermen's longshore boats and drift nets, the Coastguards' gig and the salvage yawl *Sophia*. These are in front of the tarred beach company's headquarters that was moved inland as the sea encroached. The beach company headquarters became the Fishermen's Club and had a circle cut in the wall for a telescope so that someone could always watch the boats at sea and report if any were in trouble. This Club, with its faded photographs and paintings, has survived. It was not safe for isolated communities to live on the low-lying coast at the beginning of the nineteenth century because of the French or Dutch pirates, but by about 1835 a fishing community had evolved at Beach End.

105. Eighty-two year old Stanley 'Cock Robin' Brown, left, on Kessingland beach decides 'it's too bad to go to sea today' in 1989. When 'Cock Robin' Brown first started longshore fishing in about 1921, from Beach End, Kessingland ('Kess'el to the locals), there were twenty-eight longshore 'punts' fishing from the beach. In the main autumn herring fishery they carried three men. By the early 1980s only 'Cock Robin' was doing a little part time fishing from here.

106. Fishing boats on the beach at Kessingland, 1981. In the centre is 'Cock Robin' Brown's *Result*, built in 1936 and the last of the longshore boats built at Kessingland. The company lookout and shed was at the end of Beach Road, but early in the twentieth century much of the coastal area was washed away. However the construction of a breakwater on Benacre Ness caused the shingle to build up in front of Kessingland.

Chapter Four

EASTERN ANGLES

Lowestoft and the River Waveney

107. Ruins on the seashore at Pakefield. Between 1900-30 about half the houses in the old village went over the cliff into the sea

110. A beach yawl *Happy New Year* with her normal working crew near Lowestoft Ness, the most easterly point in Britain, about 1905. These fast beach yawls (pronounced yolls) raced out to ships in distress and the first one there claimed the right to the salvage. By the time this photograph was taken steamers, which did not get into the same number of difficulties as the sailing craft, had almost put the beach companies out of work. However the fishermen continued to race their yawls and kept their fiercely independent beach companies going, often just as social clubs, until the start of World War II.

108. Above Left: The end of a house in Beach Street, Pakefield falling into the sea during a high tide in 1936. Beach Street still ends abruptly, but it was once on the inland edge of the village and led down to fishermen's huts on the shore that would now be about 500 meters out in the cold North Sea. Groynes and a concrete sea wall stopped the erosion just short of the church. There isn't a shortage of open sea, it is land that people need to live on!

109. Left: The Lowestoft Old Company shed on Lowestoft beach, 1908. The Beach Companies, which operated from every beach landing and port between Mundesley and Felixstowe Ferry, were fishermen's co-operatives involved in salvaging ships in trouble.

111. Pleasure steamer and inshore fishing boat entering Lowestoft harbour, 1900. Once, when there were no herrings inshore, the 18ft *Bessie*, an open Suffolk boat kept on Kessingland beach, sailed out to the Smith's Knoll and begged some herring from the men on a Kessingland-owned steam drifter. The boat was sailed back into Lowestoft, the herring were sold, coal collected and then sailed back to Kessingland all in one day.

112. Tripper boats being taken out to watch the sailing smacks as they were towed to sea in about 1937. The last sailing trawling smack was sold from Yarmouth in 1910, but Lowestoft still had a fleet of around 340 smacks. In 1930 there were still fifty-three smacks trawling under sail in the North Sea from Lowestoft. They kept going because they were slow-moving and used beam trawls that landed fish in better condition than the steam trawlers. Also most of the Lowestoft smacks were skipper-owned and they did not have the capital to buy expensive motor or steam vessels. The coal was expensive as Lowestoft was a long way from the coal mines. In 1939 there were still eight sailing smacks at Lowestoft, but these gave up as soon as the impact of World War II hit Britain.

24. 'Alan the Eel' Wright on his Norfolk Cruiser *Shelley* and his eel fishing boats at Iken Cliff. Alan was the last full time fisherman working just in the Alde, Ore and Butley Rivers. After twenty years of eel fishing he based the *Shelley* at Snape Maltings quay for bird-watching trips.

25. John and Graham Westrup coiling herring nets on to a 'barrow' ready to load into *Shady Nook,* the last fishing boat on Thorpeness beach, 2002. The *Shady Nook* and *Boy Bill* were built at Whisstocks from the same moulds. The fishing from Thorpeness was shrimp trawling off Sizewell, crab and lobster on the sand stone off the Ness and drift netting for herring. After Ogilvie's holiday village started the men found work ashore but went fishing when there was plenty of fish. However when fishing quotas were introduced the part time Thorpeness fishermen were not allowed to sell their catch. Mrs Wentworth turned the fishermen off the lower beach, because she thought they looked untidy, so they moved up to Ogilvie's beach. A further difficulty was caused by a sand bar formed off the beach which led to the decline of boats being kept here.

28. The *Balmoral's* first visit to the new Southwold Pier on the June 21, 2002. Chris and Irene Iredale bought Southwold Pier in 1987 and their dream of reopening it came true in 2001 when the new 610ft Southwold Pier was opened to the public. This was the first new seaside pier built in Britain for fifty years and it won the Pier of the Year Award from the National Pier Society. The following year the *Balmoral* was the first passenger vessel to visit Southwold since 1928. On the same afternoon Lady Jill Freud officially opened the T landing stage at the end of the pier.

26. Above Left: Dani Church, rowing the Southwold ferryboat across the river in 2002. During the inter-war years a rowing ferry operated between Walberswick and Southwold shore in the summer evenings after the chain ferry stopped. This was first run by Robert Cross and then, until 1937, by Ruby Cooper. The chain ferry ended at the beginning of World War II, but the Army asked 'Old Bob' Cross to revive the ferry so that soldiers based at Walberswick could cross over to Southwold. This service was continued after the war by Bob and when he retired his son Robert took over the ferry. In 1992 another member of the family, David Church, took over the rowing ferry until his early death. After this David's daughter Dani became the second lady ferryman. It was David who had decided to have a new wooden 14ft boat built for the ferry on the Black Shore, Southwold in 1998 at Harbour Marine Services.

27. Left: The model beach yawls racing at Southwold Model Yacht Regatta which with a club on the Isle of Man, is the last Victorian free style regatta, 2002. In 1892 the Town Council awarded '£5 and no more' to be spent on boarding up a yacht pond beside the Ferry Road. Two years later Mrs Vernon Hunt was organising the model yacht racing and in 1907 the Southwold Model Yacht Racing Committee was established and a Regatta has been held ever since. Another pond was built near the pier and this was enlarged in 1957. Several families have been racing model yachts at Southwold for three generations and one family has taken part for four generations.

29. Russell Upson, on the left, in the new boat building shed at Slaughden in 1990. Russell Upson had been foreman at Whisstocks, Woodbridge, but moved to Slaughden to establish his own business in 1973. On the left is a new wooden 22ft boat being built by Russell's son Bryan for D. C. Crisp to fish from Aldeburgh Beach. From the Anglo-Saxon period until this time clinker work boats were being regularly built on the eastern coast, but this boat and a few others, marked the end of 1,500 years of commercial wooden boat building.

30. Phillip 'Dodger' Holmes' *Dodger* trawling off Dunwich in 2001. Built at Knights, Woodbridge in 1991 this was the last wooden Suffolk beach boat built. The falling catches have lead the fishermen to believe that their way of life, and the traditional boats used, are moving towards extinction.

113. Lowestoft Fish Market in about 1910. In 1832 a channel for ships was dug through the shingle to Lake Lothing to form Lowestoft harbour. Norwich merchants promoted this project so that ships could bypass Yarmouth, where the merchants had the monopoly on the trade up to Norwich. The creation of Lowestoft harbour opened Norwich and Beccles up as inland ports.

114. Discharging herring at Lowestoft in 1962. Lowestoft had two different fishing communities. The drifters only worked in the summer and autumn after herring and mackerel and were mainly manned by men from the longshore fishing villages and from the farms, after harvest. While the trawlers, that mainly landed plaice, were manned by men living in the town and working all the year round.

115. **Above** The mate and three of the deck hands, on the Lowestoft drifter *Dauntless Star*, in 1962. The large-scale autumn herring fishery with drift nets was then fading out due to over-fishing and a lack of demand for herring.

116. Above Right: The inshore fishing boat *Sharon J* at the Victorian fish market, Lowestoft 1987. Most of these diesel trawlers were 'side winders', that is, the nets were pulled in over the side, but the first 'stern' trawler, *Universal Star,* had come to Lowestoft in about 1961. By 1978 Lowestoft had fifty-five 'side-winders' and fifteen stern trawlers.

117. Right: The 77ft *Excelsior*, shortly after John Wylson had brought her back from Norway, along side the Colne trawler *St Rose* in Lake Lothing, 1972. The *Excelsior* was a smack built for trawling by Chambers at Lowestoft in 1921. She was built to replace another *Excelsior*, one of the many trawlers sunk during World War I. During the 1930s the trawling smacks hardly paid their way and many were sold to Scandinavian owners. The *Excelsior* spent a period as a motor vessel carrying cargoes to the Norwegian islands.

118. The restored trawling smack *Excelsior* at the start of the Lowestoft Smack Race, 1998. In the Victorian period the trawling smacks had taken part in annual races at Lowestoft. This race had not been sailed for over a century when smacks gathered at Lowestoft to race again in 1996.

119. Above Right: Aboard the smack *Excelsior* with skipper Stuart White on the right, 1994. In 1876 Lowestoft had 348 sailing trawlers and a similar number of sailing drifters.

120. Right: Broads hire cruisers and an auxiliary sailing barge at Beccles in about 1954. Coal came up to Beccles in billyboys, the Humber barges, until 1895 and then steamers but Everard's sailing barges came up until 1939. In 1954, because of the high cost of the railways, the Beccles millers Walter Green & Sons decided to revive water transport and their Transport Manager Russell Garnham chartered barges from the London & Rochester Trading Co. The first barge up was the *Cabby*, skippered by Alex Rands of Pin Mill, a barge that could have loaded 160 tons but only brought 110 ton of Canadian wheat from the Royal Docks so that she could reach Beccles. As Green's mill was at the back of the town, the wheat had to be taken by lorry from the waterfront. About twenty different barges came up, but the most regular was the *George & Eliza* which only loaded 100 tons and went through Mutford Lock, while the bigger barges had to go around by Yarmouth.

121. A wherry berthed at Bungay. An Act was passed in 1670 that allowed the River Waveney to be fitted with locks so that freights could be taken up to Bungay. The Waveney had probably been used for cargoes before this because the Town Store House, pulled down in the 1970s, had been a fourteenth century building near the river. By the end of the nineteenth century there were three cuts leading up to staithes. By then the Bungay millers W. D. & A. E. Walker owned the navigation. One of the surviving wherries, the *Albion*, was built for them.

122. The wherry yacht *Olive* passing the pleasure wherry *Hathor* to come alongside the Waveney Hotel, Beccles, 2000. This was part of the Broads Authority's policy of hiring three wherries to move to different staithes around the Broads in the summer to give pleasure trips.

Also from Creekside Publishing by Robert Simper.

English Estuaries Series

DEBEN RIVER
RIVER ORWELL AND RIVER STOUR
RIVERS ALDE, ORE AND BLYTH
NORFOLK RIVERS AND HARBOURS
ESSEX RIVERS AND CREEKS
THAMES TIDEWAY
RIVER MEDWAY AND THE SWALE
RIVERS TO THE FENS

The Sea and the Land books
IN SEARCH OF SAIL
FAMILY FIELDS
VOYAGE AROUND EAST ANGLIA
WOODBRIDGE & BEYOND

The Coast in the Past Series
FORGOTTEN COAST

123. The Trawl Dock at Lowestoft in 1996 was empty apart from some visiting smacks. Across the harbour is the Edwardian Clubhouse of the hospitable Royal Norfolk and Suffolk Yacht Club, a racing club established in 1852.

124. The new steel brigantine *Young Endeavour* motoring into Lowestoft after her first trial sail, 1987. Brooke Marine started building the brigantine at their Lake Lothing yard, but they closed. Out of a work force of 320 people 260 were employed when Brooke Yachts International took over the completion of the *Young Endeavour*. She was built for the Government as Britain's gift to Australia to mark their Bicentenary.